# The
# BIBLE BRIEF

Read Highlights of the World's Bestselling Book
in About an Hour

BARBOUR
PUBLISHING

© 2007 by Barbour Publishing, Inc.

Compiled by Tracy Sumner, with editorial assistance by
Lauren Schneider.

ISBN 978-1-59789-758-7

Published by Barbour Publishing, Inc., P.O. Box 719,
Uhrichsville, Ohio 44683, www.barbourbooks.com

*Our mission is to publish and distribute inspirational
products offering exceptional value and biblical
encouragement to the masses.*

Member of the
Evangelical Christian
Publishers Association

Printed in the United States of America.

## *You need to know the Bible.*

The Bible influences much of our daily experience. Laws are based on its principles. Cultures are built on its foundation. People are changed by its power.

It's not surprising that a book with such impact is large and complex. Yet the major themes of the Bible—of man's sin and need, of God's power and love—are easily grasped. Sometimes, you just need to dig down to the heart of the story.

That's what *The Bible Brief* does for you. All sixty-six books of the Bible are represented here, in extremely condensed form. The major stories and themes of the Bible are distilled into a quick and easy-to-read format, which will give you a basic overview of scripture in about an hour's reading. This book is a highly-abridged version of a respected and beloved translation of the Bible—every word is from the King James Version, in its proper order. But these Bible highlights are presented in only a fraction of the King James Version's total word count.

*The Bible Brief* is not intended to replace your own personal Bible reading and study—we encourage you to pursue that regularly with a complete copy of the scripture. But our hope is that this little book will whet your appetite for greater biblical knowledge, as it gives you a helpful perspective on what the Bible is all about.

THE EDITORS

# GENESIS

In the beginning God created heaven and earth.

God said, Let us make man in our image;
male and female. God blessed them and said, Be
fruitful, replenish the earth: have dominion over
every living thing.

God saw every thing he had made, and it was
very good. On the seventh day God rested. God
blessed the seventh day and sanctified it.

The LORD put man into the garden of Eden and
commanded, Of the tree of the knowledge of
good and evil, thou shalt not eat: in the day thou
eatest thereof thou shalt die.

Now the serpent said unto the woman, Ye
shall not die: your eyes shall be opened, and ye
shall be as gods. The woman took the fruit and
did eat, and gave also unto her husband.

God said unto the serpent, Thou art cursed.
I will put enmity between thee and the woman,
between thy seed and her seed. Unto Adam
he said, In sweat shalt thou eat bread, till thou
return unto the ground; dust thou art, unto dust
shalt thou return.

God looked upon the earth, and it was corrupt.

God said unto Noah, I will destroy the earth. Make an ark. Of every living thing, two of every sort bring into the ark, to keep them alive. Noah went in, and his sons, his wife, and his sons' wives, because of the flood. All flesh died, fowl, cattle, beast, every creeping thing, and every man.

It came to pass, the waters dried up. God spake unto Noah, Go forth of the ark. Bring with thee every living thing, that they may multiply upon the earth. I set my bow in the cloud, a token of a covenant between me and the earth. I will remember my covenant, and waters shall no more become a flood to destroy all flesh.

Shem, Ham, and Japheth: these are the sons of Noah: by these were the nations divided after the flood.

The whole earth was of one language. They said one to another, Let us build a city and a tower, whose top may reach unto heaven; let us make a name, lest we be scattered upon the earth.

The LORD said, Now nothing will be restrained from them which they have imagined. Let us go down and confound their language. Therefore is the name of it Babel; because the LORD did confound the language of all the earth: and from thence did the LORD scatter them.

Terah begat Abram in Ur of the Chaldees. The LORD said unto Abram, Get out of thy country, from thy kindred, unto a land I will shew thee: I will make of thee a great nation; thou shalt be a blessing: I will bless them that bless thee and curse him that curseth thee. So Abram departed and took Sarai his wife. Abram dwelled in the land of Canaan.

The word of the LORD came unto Abram, saying, Fear not: I am thy shield, thy exceeding great reward.

Abram said, God, what wilt thou give me, seeing I go childless?

The word of the LORD came, saying, He that shall come forth out of thine own bowels shall be thine heir. Look toward heaven, and tell the stars, if thou be able to number them: so shall thy seed be.

He believed the LORD; and he counted it to him for righteousness.

The LORD did unto Sarah as he had spoken. Sarah bare Abraham a son in his old age, at the set time of which God had spoken to him. Abraham called the name of his son Isaac.

Isaac was forty years old when he took Rebekah to wife. Isaac intreated the LORD for his wife,

because she was barren: and Rebekah conceived.
When her days to be delivered were fulfilled,
behold, there were twins in her womb. The first
came out red; they called his name Esau. After
that came his brother out, and his hand took hold
on Esau's heel; his name was called Jacob.

Jacob served seven years for Rachel; they seemed
unto him but a few days for the love he had to her.
Jacob said unto Laban, Give me my wife, for my
days are fulfilled.

God remembered Rachel and opened her womb.
She bare a son and called his name Joseph.

It came to pass, when Joseph was come unto his
brethren, that they stript Joseph out of his coat and
cast him into a pit. They sat down to eat bread:
they looked, and, behold, a company of Ishmeelites
came from Gilead with camels bearing spicery and
balm and myrrh, going down to Egypt.

Judah said unto his brethren, What profit is
it if we slay our brother and conceal his blood?
Let us sell him to the Ishmeelites, and let not
our hand be upon him; for he is our brother. And
his brethren were content. They drew Joseph out
of the pit and sold Joseph to the Ishmeelites for
twenty pieces of silver: and they brought Joseph
into Egypt.

The LORD was with Joseph, and he was prosperous. At the end of two years, Pharaoh dreamed. Pharaoh said unto Joseph, I have a dream, and I have heard that thou canst interpret it. Joseph said, God hath shewed Pharaoh what he is about to do: there come seven years of great plenty, and after them seven years of famine. Pharaoh said, there is none so wise as thou: See, I have set thee over all the land of Egypt.

When Jacob saw there was corn in Egypt, Jacob said unto his sons, Behold, I have heard there is corn in Egypt: for us from thence; that we may live. And Joseph's ten brethren went down to buy corn in Egypt.

Joseph said unto his brethren, Fear not: am I in the place of God? Ye thought evil against me; but God meant it unto good, to save much people. I will nourish you and your little ones. He comforted them and spake kindly unto them.

Joseph dwelt in Egypt, he and his father's house: and lived an hundred and ten years.

# Exodus

The king of Egypt died: and the children of Israel sighed by reason of bondage. God heard their groaning and remembered his covenant with Abraham, Isaac, and Jacob.

Now Moses kept the flock of Jethro his father-in-law: he led the flock to the backside of the desert and came to the mountain of God, Horeb. The angel of the LORD appeared in a flame of fire out of the midst of a bush: and, behold, the bush burned with fire and was not consumed. Moses said, I will turn aside and see this great sight, why the bush is not burnt.

God called unto him out of the bush and said, Moses.

He said, Here am I.

And he said, Draw not nigh: put off thy shoes from thy feet, for the place whereon thou stand is holy ground. I have surely seen the affliction of my people in Egypt and have heard their cry by reason of their taskmasters. I know their sorrows; I am come down to deliver them out of the hand of the Egyptians and to bring them out of that land unto a land flowing with milk and honey. Certainly I will be with thee; and this shall be a token that I have sent thee: When thou hast brought forth the people out of Egypt, ye shall serve God upon this mountain.

Afterward Moses and Aaron went in and told Pharaoh, Thus saith the Lord God of Israel, Let my people go, that they may hold a feast unto me in the wilderness.

Pharaoh said, Who is the Lord, that I should obey his voice to let Israel go? I know not the Lord, neither will I let Israel go.

Moses returned unto the Lord and said, Wherefore hast thou so evil entreated this people? why is it that thou hast sent me? For since I came to Pharaoh to speak in thy name, he hath done evil to this people; neither hast thou delivered thy people at all.

The Lord said, Now shalt thou see what I will do to Pharaoh: for with a strong hand shall he let them go and drive them out of his land. I will harden Pharaoh's heart and multiply my signs and wonders in Egypt. But Pharaoh shall not hearken unto you, that I may lay my hand upon Egypt and bring forth my people the children of Israel out of Egypt by great judgments.

Moses called for all the elders of Israel and said,

Take a lamb according to your families, and kill the passover. Take a bunch of hyssop, dip it in the blood, and strike the lintel and two side posts; none of you shall go out the door of his house until morning. For the LORD will pass through to smite the Egyptians; when he seeth the blood upon the lintel, the LORD will pass over the door and not suffer the destroyer to smite you.

It came to pass that at midnight the LORD smote all the firstborn in Egypt, from the firstborn of Pharaoh on his throne unto the firstborn of the captive in the dungeon; and all the firstborn of cattle. Pharaoh rose up in the night, he and his servants and all the Egyptians; there was a great cry in Egypt; for there was not a house where there was not one dead. He called for Moses and Aaron by night and said, Get forth from among my people, both ye and the children of Israel; go, serve the LORD, as ye have said. Also take your flocks and herds, and be gone; and bless me also.

Thus did all the children of Israel; as the LORD commanded Moses and Aaron, so did they. It came to pass the selfsame day that the LORD did bring the children of Israel out of Egypt.

The LORD came down upon mount Sinai: and called Moses. God spake, saying, Thou shalt have no other gods before me. Thou shalt not make any graven image. Thou shalt not take the name of the LORD thy God in vain. Remember the sabbath day, to keep it holy. Honour thy father and thy mother. Thou shalt not kill. Thou shalt not commit adultery. Thou shalt not steal. Thou shalt not bear false witness. Thou shalt not covet any thing that is thy neighbour's.

# LEVITICUS

Walk in my statutes and keep my commandments; then I will give you rain in due season, and the land shall yield her increase and the trees their fruit. Your threshing shall reach unto the vintage, and the vintage shall reach unto the sowing time: ye shall eat your bread to the full and dwell in your land safely. I will give peace in the land, and ye shall lie down, and none shall make you afraid: I will rid evil beasts out of the land, neither shall the sword go through your land. Ye shall chase your enemies, and they shall fall before you by the sword. Five of you shall chase an hundred, and an hundred of you shall put ten thousand to flight.

I will have respect unto you, multiply you, and establish my covenant with you. I set my tabernacle among you: my soul shall not abhor you. I will walk among you and be your God, and ye shall be my people. I am the LORD your God, which brought you out of Egypt, that ye should not be their bondmen; I have broken the bands of your yoke and made you go upright.

But if ye will not hearken unto me and do all these commandments; if ye shall despise my statutes, or if your soul abhor my judgments so that ye break my covenant: I will do this unto you; I will appoint over you terror, consumption, and the burning ague that shall consume the eyes and cause sorrow of heart: and ye shall sow your seed in vain, for your enemies shall eat it. I will set my face against you, and ye shall be slain before your enemies: they that hate you shall reign over you; and ye shall flee when none pursueth you.

And if ye will not yet for all this hearken unto me, I will punish you seven times more for your sins. I will break the pride of your power; I will make your heaven as iron and your earth as brass: your strength shall be spent in vain: for your land shall not yield her increase, neither shall the trees yield their fruits.

# NUMBERS

The LORD spake to Moses in the wilderness of Sinai, in the tabernacle of the congregation, on the first day of the second month in the second year after they were come out of Egypt, saying, Take the sum of all the congregation of the children of Israel, after their families, by the house of their fathers, with the number of their names, every male by their polls; from twenty years old and upward, all that are able to go forth to war in Israel: thou and Aaron shall number them by their armies.

It came to pass on the twentieth day of the second month in the second year that the cloud was taken up from the tabernacle of the testimony. The children of Israel took their journeys out of the wilderness of Sinai; and the cloud rested in the wilderness of Paran.

The LORD spake unto Moses, saying, Send thou men, that they may search the land of Canaan, which I give unto the children of Israel: of every tribe of their fathers shall ye send a man, every one a ruler among them.

Moses sent them to spy out the land of

Canaan and said, Get this way southward, and go up into the mountain: see the land, what it is, and the people that dwelleth therein, whether they be strong or weak, few or many.

They returned from searching the land after forty days. They came to Moses, Aaron, and all the congregation of the children of Israel, unto the wilderness of Paran, and brought back word unto them and shewed them the fruit of the land. They said, We came unto the land whither thou sentest us, and surely it floweth with milk and honey; this is the fruit of it. Nevertheless the people be strong that dwell in the land, and the cities are walled and very great.

Caleb stilled the people before Moses and said, Let us go up at once and possess it; for we are well able to overcome it.

But the men that went up with him said, We be not able to go up against the people; for they are stronger than we.

All the children of Israel murmured against Moses and Aaron: the whole congregation said to them, Would God that we had died in Egypt! or in this wilderness! Hath the LORD brought us unto this land to fall by the sword, that our wives and children should be prey? were it not better for us to return into Egypt? They said one to another, Let us make a captain and return into Egypt.

The LORD said to Moses, How long will this

people provoke me? how long will it be ere they believe me, for all the signs I have shewed among them? I will smite them with the pestilence and disinherit them, and will make of thee a greater nation and mightier than they.

Moses said, Then the Egyptians shall hear it and tell the inhabitants of this land: for they have heard that thou art among this people, that thy cloud standeth over them, and that thou goest before them by day in a pillar of cloud, and in a pillar of fire by night.

I beseech thee, let the power of my lord be great, as thou hast spoken, saying, The LORD is longsuffering and of great mercy, forgiving iniquity and transgression. Pardon, I beseech thee, the iniquity of this people according unto the greatness of thy mercy.

The LORD said, I have pardoned according to thy word: but as truly as I live, all the earth shall be filled with the glory of the LORD. Because all those men have seen my glory and my miracles, which I did in Egypt and the wilderness, and tempted me now these ten times and not hearkened to my voice; surely they shall not see the land I sware unto their fathers, neither shall any of them that provoked me see it: but my servant Caleb, because he had another spirit with him and hath followed me fully, him will I bring into the land whereinto he went.

# DEUTERONOMY

In the fortieth year, in the eleventh month, on the first day of the month, Moses spake unto the children of Israel according unto all the LORD had given him in commandment unto them. On this side Jordan, in the land of Moab, began Moses to declare this law.

Take heed to thyself, and keep thy soul diligently, lest thou forget the things thine eyes have seen, lest they depart from thy heart all the days of thy life: but teach them thy sons and thy sons' sons; specially the day thou stoodest before the LORD thy God in Horeb, when the LORD said unto me, Gather the people together, and I will make them hear my words, that they may learn to fear me all the days they live upon the earth, and that they may teach their children.

Take heed unto yourselves, lest ye forget the covenant of the LORD your God, which he made with you, and make a graven image or the likeness of any thing, which the LORD hath forbidden thee. Remember thou wast a servant in the land of Egypt, and the LORD brought thee out thence through a mighty hand and stretched out arm: therefore the LORD commanded thee to keep the sabbath day.

Thou shalt remember the way the LORD

led thee these forty years in the wilderness, to humble thee, to prove thee, to know what was in thine heart, whether thou wouldest keep his commandments.

He suffered thee to hunger and fed thee with manna, which thou knewest not, neither did thy fathers know; that he might make thee know that man doth not live by bread only, but by every word that proceedeth out of the mouth of the LORD.

Thy raiment waxed not old upon thee, neither did thy foot swell these forty years. Thou shalt also consider in thine heart that as a man chasteneth his son, so the LORD thy God chasteneth thee. Therefore thou shalt keep the commandments of the LORD, to walk in his ways and to fear him.

Forget not how thou provokedst the LORD to wrath in the wilderness: from the day thou didst depart out of Egypt until ye came unto this place, ye have been rebellious against the LORD.

Moses the servant of the LORD died there in the land of Moab, according to the word of the LORD. And he buried him in a valley in the land of Moab.

Moses was an hundred and twenty years old when he died. And Joshua son of Nun was full of the spirit of wisdom; for Moses had laid his hands upon him: the children of Israel hearkened unto him and did as the LORD commanded Moses.

## JOSHUA

After the death of Moses, the LORD spake unto Joshua, Moses' minister, saying, Moses my servant is dead; therefore arise, go over Jordan, and all this people, unto the land I give to them.

Every place the sole of your foot shall tread upon, that have I given unto you, as I said unto Moses. There shall not any man be able to stand before thee all the days of thy life: as I was with Moses, so I will be with thee: I will not fail thee nor forsake thee.

Then Joshua commanded the officers of the people, saying, Pass through the host and command the people, Prepare victuals; for within three days ye shall pass over Jordan to go in to possess the land the LORD giveth you.

To the Reubenites, the Gadites, and half the tribe of Manasseh spake Joshua, saying, Remember the word Moses commanded you, saying, The LORD your God hath given you rest and hath given you this land.

They answered Joshua, All that thou commandest us we will do, and whithersoever thou sendest us, we will go.

A long time after the LORD had given rest unto Israel from all their enemies round about, Joshua waxed old. Joshua called for all Israel and for their elders, heads, judges, and officers and said unto them, I am stricken in age: ye have seen all that the LORD hath done unto all these nations because of you; for the LORD your God hath fought for you.

Behold, I have divided unto you by lot these nations that remain, to be an inheritance for your tribes, from Jordan, with all the nations I have cut off, even unto the great sea westward.

# JUDGES

When Joshua had let the people go, the children of Israel went every man unto his inheritance to possess the land. The people served the LORD all the days of Joshua and all the days of the elders that outlived Joshua. And Joshua died, being an hundred and ten years old. All that generation were gathered unto their fathers: and there arose another generation after them, which knew not the LORD, nor yet the works he had done for Israel.

The children of Israel did evil in the sight of

the LORD and served Baalim: they forsook the God of their fathers. The anger of the LORD was hot against Israel, and he delivered them into the hands of their enemies round about.

Nevertheless the LORD raised up judges, which delivered them out of the hand of those that spoiled them. Yet they would not hearken unto their judges, but went after other gods and bowed themselves to them: they turned quickly out of the way their fathers walked in.

The children of Israel did evil: and the LORD delivered them into the hand of Midian seven years. Israel was greatly impoverished because of the Midianites; and the children of Israel cried to the LORD. There came an angel of the LORD and sat under an oak in Ophrah, that pertained unto Joash the Abiezrite: his son Gideon threshed wheat by the winepress to hide it from the Midianites. The angel of the LORD appeared unto him and said, The LORD is with thee, mighty man of valour.

Gideon said, Oh my Lord, if the LORD be with us, why then is all this befallen us? and where be all his miracles which our fathers told us of, saying, Did not the LORD bring us up from Egypt? but now the LORD hath forsaken us and delivered us into the hands of the Midianites.

The LORD looked upon him and said, Go in

this thy might, and thou shalt save Israel from
the hand of the Midianites: have not I sent thee?

It came to pass, as soon as Gideon was dead,
the children of Israel turned again, and went a
whoring after Baalim. In those days there was no
king in Israel: every man did that which was right
in his own eyes.

## RUTH

When the judges ruled, there was a famine. A
man went to Moab, he, his wife, and two sons.
Elimelech died; Mahlon and Chilion died also.

Naomi said unto her daughters-in-law, Go,
return each to her mother's house.

Ruth said, Intreat me not to leave: whither
thou goest, I will go; thy people shall be my
people, thy God my God.

So Naomi returned, and Ruth the Moabitess
with her, to Bethlehem in the beginning of
harvest. Naomi had a kinsman of wealth; his
name was Boaz.

Ruth said, Let me go to the field and glean.

Boaz commanded his men, saying, Let her
glean even among the sheaves, reproach her not.

Naomi said, Blessed be he of the LORD, who hath not left off his kindness. The man is one of our next kinsmen.

Boaz said, I do the part of a kinsman to thee. So Boaz took Ruth, and she was his wife: and she bare a son. They called his name Obed: he is the father of Jesse, the father of David.

# 1 SAMUEL

All Israel from Dan to Beersheba knew Samuel was established to be a prophet of the LORD. The LORD appeared again in Shiloh: for the LORD revealed himself to Samuel in Shiloh by the word of the LORD.

All the elders of Israel gathered together and came to Samuel and said, Behold, thou art old, and thy sons walk not in thy ways: now make us a king to judge us like all the nations.

But the thing displeased Samuel, when they said, Give us a king. Samuel prayed unto the LORD. And the LORD said unto Samuel, Hearken unto the voice of the people: for they have not rejected thee but have rejected me, that I should not reign over them.

Now the LORD had told Samuel a day before Saul

came, Tomorrow about this time I will send a man out of the land of Benjamin, and thou shalt anoint him to be captain over my people Israel, that he may save my people out of the hand of the Philistines: for I have looked upon my people, because their cry is come unto me. When Samuel saw Saul, the LORD said, Behold the man I spake to thee of!

When he had reigned two years over Israel, Saul chose three thousand men of Israel; two thousand were with Saul in Michmash and in mount Bethel, and a thousand were with Jonathan in Gibeah: the rest of the people he sent every man to his tent.

Jonathan smote the garrison of the Philistines in Geba, and the Philistines heard of it. Saul blew the trumpet throughout all the land, saying, Let the Hebrews hear.

Saul said, Bring hither a burnt offering to me, and peace offerings. As soon as he had made an end of offering the burnt offering, Samuel came and said, What hast thou done?

Saul said, Because I saw that the people were scattered from me, and that thou camest not within the days appointed, and that the Philistines gathered at Michmash; therefore said I, The Philistines will come down now upon me to Gilgal, and I have not made supplication unto the LORD: I forced myself therefore and offered a burnt offering.

Samuel said to Saul, Thou hast done foolishly: thou hast not kept the commandment of the LORD thy God: for now would the LORD have established thy kingdom upon Israel for ever. But now thy kingdom shall not continue: the LORD hath sought a man after his own heart and commanded him to be captain over his people, because thou hast not kept that which the LORD commanded thee.

The LORD said unto Samuel, How long wilt thou mourn for Saul, seeing I have rejected him from reigning over Israel? fill thine horn with oil, and go, I will send thee to Jesse the Bethlehemite: for I have provided me a king among his sons.

Samuel took the horn of oil and anointed him in the midst of his brethren: and the Spirit of the LORD came upon David from that day forward.

# 2 SAMUEL

It came to pass that David enquired of the LORD, Shall I go up into any of the cities of Judah?

The LORD said unto him, Go up.

David said, Whither shall I go up?

And he said, Unto Hebron.

Then came all the tribes of Israel to David unto Hebron, saying, Behold, we are thy bone and thy flesh. In time past, when Saul was king over us, thou leddest out and broughtest in Israel: and the LORD said to thee, Thou shalt feed my people Israel and be a captain over Israel. So all the elders of Israel came to Hebron; and David made a league with them before the LORD: and they anointed David king over Israel.

After the year was expired, at the time when kings go forth to battle, David sent Joab, his servants, and all Israel; they destroyed the children of Ammon and besieged Rabbah. But David tarried at Jerusalem.

In an eveningtide David arose from his bed and walked upon the roof of the king's house: from the roof he saw a woman washing herself; and the woman was very beautiful. David enquired after the woman. And one said, Is not this Bathsheba, wife of Uriah the Hittite?

David sent messengers and took her; she came in unto him, and he lay with her: and she returned to her house. The woman conceived and sent and told David, I am with child.

David wrote a letter to Joab, saying, Set Uriah in the forefront of the hottest battle, and retire from him, that he may die. And there fell some of the servants of David; and Uriah the Hittite died also. When the wife of Uriah heard that her husband was dead, she mourned. When the mourning was past, David fetched her to his house, and she became his wife and bare him a son. But the thing David had done displeased the LORD.

David said unto Nathan, I have sinned against the LORD.

Nathan said, The LORD hath put away thy sin; thou shalt not die. Howbeit, because by this deed thou hast given great occasion to the enemies of the LORD to blaspheme, the child born unto thee shall surely die.

David said unto his servants, Is the child dead? They said, He is. David comforted Bathsheba, and went and lay with her: she bare a son, and called his name Solomon: and the LORD loved him.

# 1 KINGS

The days of David drew nigh that he should die; he charged Solomon his son, saying, I go the way of all the earth: be strong therefore, and shew thyself a man; keep the charge of the LORD thy God, to walk in his ways, to keep his statutes, commandments, judgments, and testimonies, as it is written in the law of Moses, that thou mayest prosper in all thou doest.

So David slept with his fathers and was buried in the city of David. The days that David reigned over Israel were forty years: seven years reigned he in Hebron, thirty-three years in Jerusalem. Then sat Solomon upon the throne of David; and his kingdom was established greatly.

Solomon loved the LORD, walking in the statutes of David his father: only he sacrificed and burnt incense in high places. The king went to Gibeon to sacrifice there. In Gibeon the LORD appeared to Solomon in a dream and said, Ask what I shall give thee.

Solomon said, Give thy servant an understanding heart to judge thy people, that I may discern between good and bad.

God said, Because thou hast not asked for long life; neither riches for thyself, nor the life of thine enemies; but for thyself understanding to discern judgment; behold, I have done according to thy words: I have given thee a wise and understanding heart.

It came to pass in the four hundred eightieth year after the children of Israel were come out of Egypt, in the fourth year of Solomon's reign over Israel, that he began to build the house of the LORD.

When Solomon was old, his wives turned away his heart after other gods: and his heart was not perfect with the LORD, as was the heart of David his father. Solomon did evil and went not fully after the LORD.

The time that Solomon reigned in Jerusalem over all Israel was forty years. Solomon slept with his fathers and was buried in the city of David: Rehoboam his son reigned in his stead.

The king answered the people roughly, saying, My father made your yoke heavy, and I will add to your yoke: my father chastised you with whips, I will chastise you with scorpions. When all Israel saw that the king hearkened not unto them, the people answered, saying, What portion have we in David?

So Israel departed unto their tents. But as for the children of Israel in the cities of Judah, Rehoboam reigned over them.

# 2 KINGS

In the twelfth year of Ahaz king of Judah began Hoshea to reign in Samaria over Israel nine years. He did evil in the sight of the LORD, but not as the kings of Israel before him. Against him came up Shalmaneser king of Assyria. The king of Assyria came throughout all the land and went up to Samaria and besieged it three years. In the ninth year of Hoshea the king of Assyria took Samaria, carried Israel away into Assyria, and placed them in the cities of the Medes.

For the children of Israel had sinned against the LORD, which had brought them up out of Egypt, from under the hand of Pharaoh, and had feared other gods and walked in the statutes of the heathen, whom the LORD cast out from before the children of Israel, and of the kings of Israel, which they had made.

Josiah was eight years old when he began to reign, and he reigned thirty-one years in Jerusalem. He did that which was right in the sight of the LORD, walked in all the way of David his father, and turned not aside to the right or to the left.

The king sent, and they gathered unto him all the elders of Judah and Jerusalem. The king went up into the house of the LORD, and all the men of Judah and all the inhabitants of Jerusalem with him, the priests, prophets, and all the people, both small and great: he read in their ears all the words of the book of the covenant which was found in the house of the LORD.

The king stood by a pillar and made a covenant before the LORD, to walk after the LORD and to keep his commandments with all their heart and soul, to perform the words of this covenant that were written in this book. And all the people stood to the covenant.

Notwithstanding the LORD turned not from the fierceness of his great wrath, wherewith his anger was kindled against Judah, because of all the provocations that had provoked him withal. The LORD said, I will remove Judah also out of my sight, as I have removed Israel, and will cast off this city Jerusalem which I have chosen, and the house of which I said, My name shall be there.

Jehoiachin was eighteen years old when he began to reign, and he reigned in Jerusalem three months. He did evil in the sight of the LORD, according to all his father had done.

At that time Nebuchadnezzar king of Babylon came against the city, and his servants did besiege it.

In the fifth month, on the seventh day of the month, which is the nineteenth year of Nebuchadnezzar king of Babylon, came Nebuzaradan, captain of the guard, a servant of the king of Babylon, unto Jerusalem: he burnt the house of the LORD, and the king's house, and all the houses of Jerusalem, and every great man's house burnt he with fire. So Judah was carried away out of their land.

# 1 CHRONICLES

David the king said unto all the congregation, Solomon my son, whom alone God hath chosen, is yet young and tender, and the work is great: for the palace is not for man but for the LORD.

Now I have prepared with all my might for the house of my God the gold for things to be made of gold, the silver for things of silver, the brass for things of brass, the iron for things of iron, and wood for things of wood; onyx stones,

stones to be set, glistering stones, and of divers colours, all manner of precious stones, and marble stones in abundance.

Moreover, because I have set my affection to the house of my God, I have of mine own gold and silver given to the house of my God over and above all I have prepared for the holy house. Who then is willing to consecrate his service this day unto the LORD?

Then the chief of the fathers and princes of the tribes of Israel and the captains of thousands and of hundreds, with the rulers of the king's work, offered willingly for the service of the house of God of gold five thousand talents and ten thousand drams, and of silver ten thousand talents, and of brass eighteen thousand talents, and one hundred thousand talents of iron.

Wherefore David blessed the LORD before all the congregation: David said, Blessed be thou, LORD God of Israel our father, for ever and ever. Thine is the greatness, the power, the glory, the victory, and the majesty: for all that is in heaven and in earth is thine; thine is the kingdom, and thou art exalted as head above all. Both riches and honour come of thee, and thou reignest over all; in thine hand is power and might; in thine hand it is to make great and to give strength unto all. Therefore we thank thee and praise thy glorious name.

# 2 Chronicles

Asa did that which was good and right in the eyes of the LORD his God: he took away the altars of the strange gods and the high places, brake down the images, and cut down the groves: and commanded Judah to seek the God of their fathers and to do the law and the commandment.

The Spirit of God came upon Azariah son of Oded: he went out to meet Asa and said, Hear me, Asa, and all Judah and Benjamin; the LORD is with you while ye be with him; if ye seek him, he will be found of you; but if ye forsake him, he will forsake you. Now for a long season Israel hath been without the true God, without a teaching priest, and without law. But when they in their trouble did turn unto the God of Israel and sought him, he was found of them. In those times there was no peace to him that went out, nor to him that came in, but great vexations were upon all the inhabitants of the countries. And nation was destroyed of nation, and city of city: for God did vex them with all adversity. Be strong therefore, and let not your hands be weak: for your work shall be rewarded.

The God of their fathers sent to them by his messengers, because he had compassion on his people and his dwelling place: but they mocked the messengers of God, despised his words, and misused his prophets, until the wrath of the LORD arose against his people, till there was no remedy. Therefore he brought upon them the king of the Chaldees, who slew their young men with the sword in the house of their sanctuary and had no compassion upon young man or maiden, old man, or him that stooped for age: he gave them all into his hand. All the vessels of the house of God, great and small, and the treasures of the house of the LORD, and the treasures of the king and of his princes; all these he brought to Babylon. They burnt the house of God, brake down the wall of Jerusalem, burnt all the palaces thereof with fire, and destroyed all the goodly vessels thereof. Them that had escaped from the sword carried he away to Babylon; where they were servants to him and his sons until the reign of the kingdom of Persia: to fulfill the word of the LORD by the mouth of Jeremiah, until the land had enjoyed her sabbaths: for as long as she lay desolate she kept sabbath, to fulfill threescore and ten years.

Now in the first year of Cyrus king of Persia, that the word of the LORD spoken by Jeremiah might be accomplished, the LORD stirred the

spirit of Cyrus, that he made a proclamation
in writing, saying, Thus saith Cyrus, All the
kingdoms of the earth hath the God of heaven
given me; and he hath charged me to build him
an house in Jerusalem. Who is there among you
of all his people? The LORD his God be with him,
and let him go.

# EZRA

Then rose up the chief of the fathers of Judah
and Benjamin, and the priests, and the Levites,
with all them whose spirit God had raised, to go
up to build the house of the LORD.

After these things, in the reign of Artaxerxes
king of Persia, Ezra son of Seraiah went up from
Babylon; he was a scribe in the law of Moses,
which the God of Israel had given: and the king
granted his request, according to the hand of the
LORD his God upon him.

For Ezra had prepared his heart to seek the
law of the LORD and to do it, and to teach in
Israel statutes and judgments.

# NEHEMIAH

The words of Nehemiah. It came to pass that
Hanani, one of my brethren, came, he and certain
men of Judah; and I asked them concerning
the Jews which were left of the captivity, and
concerning Jerusalem.

They said unto me, The remnant that are left
there in the province are in great affliction: the
wall of Jerusalem is broken down, and the gates
thereof are burned.

When I heard these words, I sat down and
wept, mourned certain days, fasted, prayed before
the God of heaven, and said, I beseech thee,
LORD God: let thine ear be attentive, that thou
may hear the prayer of thy servant.

I was the king's cupbearer. I said unto the king, If
thy servant have found favour in thy sight, send
me unto Judah, that I may build it. It pleased the
king to send me.

When the wall was built, and I had set up the
doors, I gave my brother Hanani charge over
Jerusalem: for he was a faithful man, and feared
God above many.

# ESTHER

King Ahasuerus made a feast unto all the people in Shushan. On the seventh day, when the heart of the king was merry with wine, he commanded the chamberlains to bring Vashti the queen before the king to show the people her beauty. But Vashti refused to come: therefore anger burned in the king. The king said to the wise men, What shall we do unto the queen?

Memucan answered, Let it be written that Vashti come no more before king Ahasuerus; and let the king give her royal estate unto another better than she.

Then said the king's servants, Let there be fair young virgins sought for the king: and let the maiden which pleaseth the king be queen instead of Vashti.

Now in Sushan there was a certain Jew, Mordecai. He brought up Hadassah, that is, Esther, his uncle's daughter: the maid was beautiful.

Esther was brought unto the king's house. Esther obtained favour in the sight of all that looked upon her. So Esther was taken unto Ahasuerus. The king loved Esther above all the women and made her queen. Esther had not yet shewed her kindred nor her people; as Mordecai had charged her. After these things did Ahasuerus promote Haman. Haman sought to destroy all Jews throughout the kingdom. Haman said unto Ahasuerus, There is a certain people dispersed among the people in thy kingdom; their laws are diverse from all people; neither keep they the king's laws. Let it be written that they may be destroyed.

The king said, Do with them as seemeth good to thee.

When Mordecai perceived all that was done, Mordecai rent his clothes.

Then called Esther for Hatach, one of the chamberlains, and gave him a commandment to Mordecai, to know what it was and why it was.

Mordecai gave him the copy of the decree, to shew it unto Esther and to charge her that she should go in unto the king to make request for her people.

Hatach told Esther the words of Mordecai. Esther gave him commandment unto Mordecai; Whosoever shall come unto the king, who is not called, there is one law to put him to death, except such to whom the king shall hold out the golden sceptre: but I have not been called to come in thirty days.

Mordecai commanded to answer Esther, If

thou holdest thy peace at this time, then shall there deliverance arise to the Jews from another place; but thou and thy father's house shall be destroyed: and who knoweth whether thou art come to the kingdom for such a time as this?

Esther bade them return this answer, Gather all the Jews in Shushan, and fast for me three days: I also will fast; and so will I go in unto the king: and if I perish, I perish.

On the third day, Esther stood in the inner court of the king's house. The king saw Esther and held out the sceptre in his hand. Said the king, What is thy request?

Esther answered, Let the king and Haman come this day unto the banquet I have prepared.

So the king and Haman came to banquet with Esther.

The king said, What is thy petition?

Esther answered, Let my life be given me, and my people. For we are sold to be destroyed.

The king said, Who is he that durst presume in his heart to do so?

Esther said, This wicked Haman.

Harbonah, one of the chamberlains, said before the king, Behold, the gallows, which Haman had made for Mordecai, standeth in the house of Haman.

Then the king said, Hang him thereon.

Esther stood before the king and said, Let it be written to reverse the letters devised by Haman. For how can I endure to see the evil that shall come unto my people?

The king said unto Esther and Mordecai, Write ye also for the Jews, as it liketh you, in the king's name.

The commandment was published unto all people, that the Jews should be ready against that day to avenge themselves on their enemies.

Mordecai went out from the presence of the king in royal apparel: and the city of Shushan rejoiced. Many people of the land became Jews; for the fear of the Jews fell upon them.

## JOB

Job was perfect and upright, one that feared God and eschewed evil.

The LORD said unto Satan, Hast thou considered my servant Job, that there is none like him in the earth, a perfect and upright man?

Satan answered, Doth Job fear God for nought? Hast not thou made a hedge about him, his house, and all he hath? thou hast blessed the work of his hands, and his substance is increased in the land. But put forth thine hand now and touch all he hath, and he will curse thee to thy face.

The LORD said unto Satan, Behold, all he hath is in thy power; only upon himself put not forth thine hand. So Satan went forth from the presence of the LORD.

There came a messenger unto Job and said, The oxen were plowing, and the asses feeding beside them: and the Sabeans fell upon them and took them away; yea, they have slain the servants with the sword; I only am escaped to tell thee.

While he was yet speaking, there came another and said, Thy sons and daughters were eating and drinking wine in their eldest brother's house: there came a great wind from the wilderness and smote the house, and it fell upon the young men, and they are dead; I only am escaped to tell thee.

Job arose, rent his mantle, shaved his head, fell down upon the ground, worshipped, and said, Naked came I out of my mother's womb, and naked shall I return thither: the LORD gave, and the LORD hath taken away; blessed be the name of the LORD. In all this Job sinned not, nor charged God foolishly.

The Lord said unto Satan, Hast thou considered Job? still he holdeth fast his integrity.

Satan answered, All a man hath will he give for his life. But touch his flesh, and he will curse thee to thy face.

The Lord said, Behold, he is in thine hand; but save his life.

So went Satan forth from the presence of the LORD and smote Job with boils from the sole of his foot unto his crown. He took a potsherd to scrape himself withal; and he sat down among the ashes.

After this opened Job his mouth and cursed his day. Job said, Let the day perish wherein I was born, and the night in which it was said, There is a man-child conceived. Let that day be darkness; let not God regard it from above, neither let the light shine upon it.

The LORD answered Job, Who is this that darkeneth counsel by words without knowledge? Gird up thy loins like a man; for I will demand of thee, and answer thou me.

Where wast thou when I laid the foundations of the earth? declare, if thou hast understanding. Who hath laid the measures thereof? or who hath stretched the line upon it? Whereupon are the foundations thereof fastened? or who laid the corner stone thereof; when the morning stars sang together, and all the sons of God shouted for joy?

Job answered the LORD, I know thou canst do every thing and no thought can be withholden from thee. Who is he that hideth counsel without knowledge? therefore have I uttered that I understood not; things too wonderful for me, which I knew not.

Hear, I beseech thee, and I will speak: I will demand of thee, and declare thou unto me. I have heard of thee by the hearing of the ear: but now mine eye seeth thee. Wherefore I abhor myself and repent in dust and ashes.

# PSALMS

Blessed is the man that walketh not in the counsel of the ungodly, nor standeth in the way of sinners, nor sitteth in the seat of the scornful. But his delight is in the law of the LORD; and in his law he meditates day and night. He shall be like a tree planted by rivers of water, that bringeth forth his fruit in his season; his leaf shall not wither; whatsoever he doeth shall prosper.

I will love thee, O LORD, my strength. The LORD is my rock, my fortress, and my deliverer; my God, my strength, in whom I will trust; my buckler, the horn of my salvation, and my high tower. I will call upon the LORD, who is worthy to be praised: so shall I be saved from mine enemies.

The LORD is my shepherd; I shall not want. He maketh me to lie down in green pastures: he leadeth me beside still waters. He restoreth my soul: he leadeth me in paths of righteousness for his name's sake. Yea, though I walk through the valley of the shadow of death, I will fear no evil: for thou art with me; thy rod and thy staff they comfort me. Thou preparest a table before me in the presence of mine enemies: thou anointest my head with oil; my cup runneth over. Surely goodness and mercy shall follow me all the days of my life: and I will dwell in the house of the LORD for ever.

Blessed is he whose transgression is forgiven, whose sin is covered. Blessed is the man unto whom the LORD imputeth not iniquity, and in whose spirit there is no guile. When I kept silence, my bones waxed old through my roaring all the day long. For day and night thy hand was heavy upon me: my moisture is turned into the drought of summer. I acknowledge my sin unto thee, and mine iniquity have I not hid. I said, I will confess my transgressions unto the LORD; and thou forgavest the iniquity of my sin.

Delight thyself in the LORD: and he shall give thee the desires of thine heart. Commit thy way unto the LORD; trust also in him; and he shall bring it to pass. He shall bring forth thy righteousness as the light, and thy judgment as the noonday.

As the hart panteth after the water brooks, so panteth my soul after thee, O God. My soul thirsteth for the living God: when shall I come and appear before God? My tears have been my meat day and night, while they continually say unto me, Where is thy God? When I remember these things, I pour out my soul in me: for I had gone with the multitude, I went with them to the house of God, with the voice of joy and praise, with a multitude that kept holyday.

Blessed are the undefiled in the way, who walk in the law of the LORD. Blessed are they that keep his testimonies and seek him with the whole heart. They also do no iniquity: they walk in his ways. Thou hast commanded us to keep thy precepts diligently. O that my ways were directed to keep thy statutes! Then shall I not be ashamed, when I have respect unto all thy commandments. I will praise thee with uprightness of heart, when I shall have learned thy righteous judgments. I will keep thy statutes.
　　Wherewithal shall a young man cleanse his way? by taking heed thereto according to thy word. With my whole heart have I sought thee:

let me not wander from thy commandments. Thy word have I hid in mine heart, that I might not sin against thee.

# PROVERBS

The proverbs of Solomon, son of David, king of Israel; to know wisdom and instruction; to perceive the words of understanding; to receive the instruction of wisdom, justice, judgment, and equity; to give subtilty to the simple, to the young man knowledge and discretion.

The fear of the LORD is the beginning of knowledge: but fools despise wisdom and instruction.

My son, if thou wilt receive my words and hide my commandments; so that thou incline thine ear unto wisdom and apply thine heart to understanding; yea, if thou criest after knowledge and liftest up thy voice for understanding; if thou seekest her as silver and searchest for her as for hid treasures; then shalt thou understand the fear of the LORD and find the knowledge of God. For the LORD giveth wisdom: out of his mouth cometh knowledge and understanding.

Trust in the LORD with all thine heart; lean not unto thine own understanding. In all thy ways acknowledge him, and he shall direct thy paths. Be not wise in thine own eyes: fear the LORD, and depart from evil.

Keep thy heart with all diligence; for out of it are the issues of life. Put away from thee a froward mouth and perverse lips.

A soft answer turneth away wrath: but grievous words stir up anger. The tongue of the wise useth knowledge aright: but the mouth of fools poureth out foolishness. A wholesome tongue is a tree of life: but perverseness therein is a breach in the spirit.

Who can find a virtuous woman? for her price is far above rubies. The heart of her husband doth safely trust in her so that he shall have no need of spoil. She will do him good and not evil all the days of her life.

Favour is deceitful, and beauty is vain: but a woman that feareth the LORD shall be praised. Give her of the fruit of her hands; and let her own works praise her in the gates.

# ECCLESIASTES

The words of the Preacher, son of David, king in Jerusalem.

Vanity of vanities, saith the Preacher, all is vanity. What profit hath a man of all his labour which he taketh under the sun?

I said in mine heart, I will prove thee with mirth, therefore enjoy pleasure: and, behold, this also is vanity. I said of laughter, It is mad: and of mirth, What doeth it?

Let us hear the conclusion of the whole matter: Fear God and keep his commandments: for this is the whole duty of man. God shall bring every work into judgment, with every secret thing, whether it be good or evil.

# SONG OF SOLOMON

The song of songs, which is Solomon's.

Let him kiss me with the kisses of his mouth: for thy love is better than wine.

I am the rose of Sharon and the lily of the valleys. As the lily among thorns, so is my love among the daughters. As the apple tree among the trees of the wood, so is my beloved among the sons.

He brought me to the banqueting house, and his banner over me was love.

## ISAIAH

The vision of Isaiah, son of Amoz, which he saw concerning Judah and Jerusalem in the days of Uzziah, Jotham, Ahaz, and Hezekiah, kings of Judah.

Hear, O heavens, and give ear, O earth: for the LORD hath spoken, I have nourished and brought up children, and they have rebelled against me.

Woe unto them that draw iniquity with cords of vanity, and sin as it were with a cart rope: that say, Let him hasten his work, that we may see it! Woe unto them that call evil good, and good evil; that put darkness for light, and light for darkness; that put bitter for sweet, and sweet for bitter!

Therefore as the fire devoureth the stubble and the flame consumeth the chaff, so their root shall be as rottenness and their blossom shall go up as dust: because they have cast away the law of the LORD and despised the word of the Holy

One of Israel. Therefore is the anger of the LORD kindled against his people, and he hath stretched forth his hand against them and smitten them.

In the year that king Uzziah died I saw the LORD sitting upon a throne, high and lifted up, and his train filled the temple. Above it stood the seraphims: one cried unto another and said, Holy, holy, holy is the LORD of hosts: the whole earth is full of his glory. The posts of the door moved at the voice of him that cried, and the house was filled with smoke.

Then said I, Woe is me! I am undone; because I am a man of unclean lips, and I dwell in the midst of a people of unclean lips: for mine eyes have seen the King.

Then flew one of the seraphims unto me, having a live coal in his hand, which he had taken with tongs from off the altar: he laid it upon my mouth and said, This hath touched thy lips; and thine iniquity is taken away and thy sin purged.

Also I heard the voice of the Lord, saying, Whom shall I send, and who will go for us? Then said I, Here am I; send me.

Hear now, O house of David; Is it a small thing for you to weary men, but will ye weary my God also? Therefore the Lord himself shall give you

a sign; behold, a virgin shall conceive and bear a
son and shall call his name Immanuel.

For unto us a child is born, a son is given: and
the government shall be upon his shoulder: his
name shall be called Wonderful, Counsellor, The
mighty God, The everlasting Father, The Prince
of Peace. Of the increase of his government and
peace there shall be no end, upon the throne of
David, and upon his kingdom, to order it and
to establish it with judgment and justice from
henceforth even for ever.

Who hath believed our report? and to whom is
the arm of the LORD revealed? For he shall grow
up before him as a tender plant and as a root out
of dry ground: he hath no form nor comeliness;
and when we shall see him, there is no beauty
that we should desire him.

He is despised and rejected of men; a man
of sorrows and acquainted with grief: we hid
our faces from him; he was despised, and we
esteemed him not. Surely he hath borne our
griefs and carried our sorrows: yet we did esteem
him stricken, smitten of God, and afflicted. But
he was wounded for our transgressions, he was
bruised for our iniquities.

All we like sheep have gone astray; we have
turned every one to his own way; and the LORD

hath laid on him the iniquity of us all. He was oppressed and afflicted, yet he opened not his mouth: he is brought as a lamb to the slaughter, and as a sheep before her shearers is dumb, so he openeth not his mouth.

Yet it pleased the LORD to bruise him; he hath put him to grief: when thou shalt make his soul an offering for sin, he shall see his seed, he shall prolong his days, and the pleasure of the LORD shall prosper in his hand. He shall see of the travail of his soul and be satisfied: by his knowledge shall my righteous servant justify many; for he shall bear their iniquities.

The Spirit of the Lord GOD is upon me; because the LORD hath anointed me to preach good tidings unto the meek; he hath sent me to bind up the brokenhearted, to proclaim liberty to the captives and the opening of the prison to them that are bound; to proclaim the acceptable year of the LORD and the day of vengeance of our God; to comfort all that mourn.

# JEREMIAH

The words of Jeremiah, son of Hilkiah, of the priests in Anathoth in the land of Benjamin: The word of the LORD came unto me, saying, Before I formed thee in the belly I knew thee; before thou came out of the womb I sanctified thee and ordained thee a prophet unto the nations.

Then the LORD put forth his hand and touched my mouth. The LORD said unto me, Behold, I have put my words in thy mouth.

The word of the LORD came to me, saying, Go and cry in the ears of Jerusalem, saying, Thus saith the LORD; I remember thee, the kindness of thy youth, the love of thine espousals, when thou wentest after me in the wilderness, in a land that was not sown. Israel was holiness unto the LORD and the firstfruits of his increase: all that devour him shall offend; evil shall come upon them.

Thus saith the LORD, What iniquity have your fathers found in me, that they are gone far from me and have walked after vanity and are become vain? Neither said they, Where is the LORD that brought us up out of Egypt, that led us through the wilderness, through a land of deserts and pits, through a land of drought and the shadow of death, through a land no man passed through and where no man dwelt?

If thou wilt return, O Israel, saith the LORD, return unto me: and if thou wilt put away thine abominations, then shalt thou not remove. Thou shalt swear, The LORD liveth in truth, in judgment, and in righteousness; the nations shall bless themselves in him, and in him shall they glory.

Thus saith the LORD to the men of Judah and Jerusalem, Break up your fallow ground, and sow not among thorns. Circumcise yourselves to the LORD, and take away the foreskins of your heart: lest my fury come forth like fire and burn that none can quench it, because of the evil of your doings.

How do ye say, We are wise, and the law of the LORD is with us? Certainly in vain made he it; the pen of the scribes is in vain. The wise men are ashamed, they are dismayed and taken: they have rejected the word of the LORD; what wisdom is in them? Therefore will I give their wives unto others and their fields to them that shall inherit them: for every one from the least unto the greatest is given to covetousness, from the prophet even unto the priest every one dealeth falsely.

Thus saith the LORD unto this people, Thus have they loved to wander, they have not refrained their feet, therefore the LORD doth not accept them; he will now remember their iniquity and visit their sins.

Thus saith the LORD, After seventy years be accomplished at Babylon I will visit you and perform my good word toward you, in causing you to return to this place. For I know the thoughts I think toward you, thoughts of peace and not of evil, to give you an expected end. Then shall ye call upon me and pray unto me, and I will hearken unto you. Ye shall seek me and find me when ye search for me with all your heart. I will be found of you: I will turn away your captivity and gather you from all the nations and all the places whither I have driven you; and I will bring you again into the place whence I caused you to be carried away captive.

Again there shall be heard in this place, which ye say shall be desolate, even in the cities of Judah and in the streets of Jerusalem that are desolate, without man and without beast, the voice of joy and of gladness, the voice of the bridegroom and of the bride, the voice of them that shall say, Praise the LORD of hosts: for the LORD is good; his mercy endureth for ever: and of them that shall bring the sacrifice of praise into the house of the LORD. For I will cause to return the captivity of the land, as at the first, saith the LORD.

## LAMENTATIONS

How doth the city sit solitary, that was full of people! how is she become as a widow! she that was great among the nations and princess among the provinces, how is she become tributary!

She weepeth in the night, and her tears are on her cheeks: among all her lovers she hath none to comfort her: all her friends have dealt treacherously with her, they are become her enemies.

This I recall to my mind, therefore have I hope. It is of the LORD's mercies that we are not consumed, because his compassions fail not. They are new every morning: great is thy faithfulness.

# EZEKIEL

It came to pass, as I was among the captives by the river Chebar, that the heavens were opened, and I saw visions of God.

In the fifth year of king Jehoiachin's captivity, the word of the LORD came expressly unto Ezekiel the priest, son of Buzi, in the land of the Chaldeans by the river Chebar; and the hand of the LORD was there upon him.

He said unto me, Son of man, I send thee to the children of Israel, to a rebellious nation that hath rebelled against me: they and their fathers have transgressed against me, even unto this very day. For they are impudent children and stiffhearted. I send thee unto them; thou shalt say, Thus saith the Lord GOD. And they, whether they will hear or forbear, yet shall know that there hath been a prophet among them.

Son of man, be not afraid of them, though briers and thorns be with thee and thou dost dwell among scorpions: be not afraid of their words, nor dismayed at their looks, though they be a rebellious house. Thou shalt speak my words unto them, whether they will hear or forbear: for they are most rebellious. But thou, son of man,

hear what I say unto thee; Be not rebellious like
that rebellious house: open thy mouth, and eat
that I give thee.

Again the word of the LORD came unto me,
saying, Son of man, speak to the children of thy
people and say, When I bring the sword upon a
land, if the people of the land take a man of their
coasts and set him for their watchman: if when
he seeth the sword come upon the land, he blow
the trumpet and warn the people; then whosoever
heareth the sound of the trumpet and taketh not
warning; if the sword come and take him away,
his blood shall be upon his own head.

The word of the LORD came unto me, saying,
Son of man, prophesy against the shepherds of
Israel and say, Woe to the shepherds of Israel that
feed themselves! should not the shepherds feed
the flocks? Ye eat the fat, ye clothe you with the
wool, ye kill them that are fed: but ye feed not
the flock.

Also prophesy unto the mountains of Israel and
say, Ye mountains of Israel, hear the word of the
LORD: Because the enemy hath said against you,
Aha, even the ancient high places are ours in
possession; because they have made you desolate
and swallowed you up on every side, that ye
might be a possession unto the residue of the
heathen, and ye are taken up in the lips of talkers

and are an infamy of the people: therefore hear
the word of the Lord GOD; Thus saith the Lord
GOD to the mountains, the hills, the rivers, the
valleys, the desolate wastes, and the cities that are
forsaken, which became a prey and derision to
the residue of the heathen that are round about.

## DANIEL

In the third year of the reign of Jehoiakim king
of Judah came Nebuchadnezzar king of Babylon
unto Jerusalem and besieged it. The Lord gave
Jehoiakim into his hand, with part of the vessels of
the house of God: which he carried into the land
of Shinar and into the treasure house of his god.

Nebuchadnezzar made an image of gold. Then the
princes, governors, captains, and all the rulers of
the provinces were gathered unto the dedication
of the image the king had set up. An herald cried
aloud, To you it is commanded, O people, nations,
and languages, that at what time ye hear all kinds
of musick, ye fall down and worship the image
the king hath set up: whoso falleth not down and
worshippeth shall the same hour be cast into the
midst of a fiery furnace.

At that time certain Chaldeans accused the

Jews. There are certain Jews thou hast set over the affairs of Babylon, Shadrach, Meshach, and Abednego; these men, O king, serve not thy gods, nor worship the image thou hast set up.

Nebuchadnezzar in his fury commanded to bring Shadrach, Meshach, and Abednego. They brought these men before the king. Nebuchadnezzar said, Is it true, do not ye worship the image I have set up?

Shadrach, Meshach, and Abednego answered, O Nebuchadnezzar, we are not careful to answer thee in this matter. If it be so, our God is able to deliver us from the furnace, and he will deliver us out of thine hand. But if not, be it known unto thee that we will not serve thy gods, nor worship the image thou hast set up.

Nebuchadnezzar commanded the most mighty men in his army to bind Shadrach, Meshach, and Abednego and cast them into the furnace. These three men fell down bound into the midst of the furnace. Then the king was astonied and said, I see four men loose, walking in the fire, and they have no hurt; and the fourth is like the Son of God.

Darius the Median took the kingdom. It pleased Darius to set over the kingdom three presidents; of whom Daniel was first. An excellent spirit was in him; and the king thought to set him over the whole realm. The presidents and princes sought to find occasion against Daniel concerning the kingdom; but they could find none. Then said these men, We shall not find any occasion against this Daniel, except we find it concerning the law of his God.

These presidents and princes assembled to the king and said, King Darius, establish a royal statute that whoever shall ask a petition of any God or man for thirty days, save of thee, shall be cast into the den of lions.

King Darius signed the decree.

When Daniel knew the writing was signed, he went into his house; his windows being open toward Jerusalem, he prayed and gave thanks before his God, as he did aforetime.

Then these men found Daniel praying and said before the king, Daniel regardeth not the decree thou hast signed.

The king, when he heard these words, was displeased with himself and set his heart on Daniel to deliver him.

These men said unto the king, No decree which the king establisheth may be changed.

Then the king commanded, and they brought Daniel and cast him into the den of lions. The king said unto Daniel, Thy God whom thou servest continually will deliver thee.

The king arose very early in the morning and

went unto the den of lions. He said, Daniel, is thy God able to deliver thee from the lions?

Then said Daniel, My God hath sent his angel and shut the lions' mouths, they have not hurt me.

Then was the king exceeding glad and commanded they take Daniel out of the den. The king commanded, and they brought those men which had accused Daniel and cast them into the den; and the lions had mastery of them.

King Darius wrote unto all people, I make a decree, That in every dominion of my kingdom men fear the God of Daniel: he is the living God, and his dominion shall be even unto the end.

# HOSEA

The word of the LORD that came unto Hosea son of Beeri in the days of Uzziah, Jotham, Ahaz, and Hezekiah, kings of Judah, and in the days of Jeroboam son of Joash, king of Israel.

The LORD said to Hosea, Go, take unto thee a wife of whoredoms and children of whoredoms: for the land hath committed great whoredom, departing from the LORD.

Then said the LORD unto me, Go, love a woman beloved of her friend, yet an adulteress, according to the love of the LORD toward the children of Israel, who look to other gods.

Hear the word of the LORD, children of Israel: for the LORD hath a controversy with the inhabitants of the land, because there is no truth nor mercy nor knowledge of God in the land.

## JOEL

The word of the LORD that came to Joel, son of Pethuel.

Hear this, old men, and give ear, all inhabitants of the land. That which the palmerworm hath left hath the locust eaten; and that which the locust hath left hath the cankerworm eaten; and that which the cankerworm hath left hath the caterpiller eaten.

I will restore to you the years that the locust hath eaten, the cankerworm, caterpiller, and palmerworm, my great army which I sent among you. Ye shall eat in plenty and be satisfied and praise the name of the LORD your God.

# Amos

The days come, saith the LORD, that the plowman shall overtake the reaper, and the treader of grapes him that soweth seed; the mountains shall drop sweet wine, and all the hills shall melt.

I will bring again the captivity of my people of Israel, and they shall build the waste cities and inhabit them; they shall plant vineyards and drink the wine thereof; they shall make gardens and eat the fruit of them.

I will plant them upon their land, and they shall no more be pulled up out of their land I have given them, saith the LORD.

# Obadiah

The vision of Obadiah concerning Edom: For thy violence against thy brother Jacob shame shall cover thee, and thou shalt be cut off for ever.

# JONAH

The word of the LORD came unto Jonah, saying,
Go to Nineveh and cry against it, for their
wickedness. But Jonah rose to flee from the
presence of the LORD and found a ship going to
Tarshish.

The LORD sent a great wind so the ship was
like to be broken. The mariners were afraid and
said, What shall we do unto thee, that the sea
may be calm?

He said, Cast me into the sea; for I know that
for my sake this tempest is upon you.

Now the LORD had prepared a great fish to
swallow Jonah. Jonah was in the fish three days.

Then Jonah prayed, and the LORD spake unto
the fish, and it vomited Jonah upon dry land.
Jonah arose, went unto Nineveh, and cried, Yet
forty days, and Nineveh shall be overthrown. The
people believed God. And God saw that they
turned from their evil way.

But it displeased Jonah exceedingly. Then said
the LORD, Should not I spare Nineveh, wherein are
more than sixscore thousand persons?

# MICAH

I will look unto the LORD; I will wait for the
God of my salvation. Rejoice not against me,
O mine enemy: when I fall, I shall arise; when
I sit in darkness, the LORD shall be a light unto
me. I will bear the indignation of the LORD,
because I have sinned against him, until he plead
my cause and execute judgment for me: he will
bring me forth to the light, and I shall behold his
righteousness.

What doth the LORD require of thee but to do
justly, love mercy, and walk humbly with thy
God?

# NAHUM

The LORD is slow to anger and great in power
and will not at all acquit the wicked: the LORD
hath his way in the whirlwind and in the storm,
and the clouds are the dust of his feet.

# HABAKKUK

The fig tree shall not blossom, neither shall fruit be in the vines; the labour of the olive shall fail, and the fields yield no meat; the flock shall be cut off from the fold, and there shall be no herd in the stalls: Yet I will rejoice in the LORD, I will joy in the God of my salvation.

# ZEPHANIAH

Seek ye the LORD, all ye meek of the earth, which have wrought his judgment; seek righteousness, seek meekness: it may be ye shall be hid in the day of the LORD's anger.

# HAGGAI

Is the seed yet in the barn? yea, as yet the vine, fig tree, pomegranate, and olive tree hath not brought forth: from this day will I bless you.

# ZECHARIAH

In the second year of Darius came the word of the LORD unto Zechariah, saying, The LORD hath been displeased with your fathers. Therefore say unto them, Thus saith the LORD; Turn unto me, and I will turn unto you.

Thus speaketh the LORD, saying, Execute true judgment, shew mercy and compassions every man to his brother: oppress not the widow, nor the fatherless, the stranger, nor the poor; and let none of you imagine evil against his brother in your heart. But they stopped their ears, that they should not hear. Yea, they made their hearts as an adamant stone, lest they should hear the words the LORD of hosts sent by the former prophets: therefore came a great wrath from the LORD.

# MALACHI

Behold, the day cometh that shall burn as an oven; all the proud and all that do wickedly shall be stubble. But unto you that fear my name shall the Sun of righteousness arise with healing in his wings.

# MATTHEW

Now the birth of Jesus Christ was on this wise:
When his mother Mary was espoused to Joseph,
before they came together, she was found with
child of the Holy Ghost. Joseph her husband,
being a just man and not willing to make her
a public example, was minded to put her away
privily.

But while he thought on these things, the
angel of the Lord appeared unto him in a dream,
saying, Joseph, son of David, fear not to take
Mary thy wife: for that which is conceived in her
is of the Holy Ghost. She shall bring forth a son,
and thou shalt call his name JESUS: for he shall
save his people from their sins.

All this was done, that it might be fulfilled
which was spoken of the Lord by the prophet,
saying, Behold, a virgin shall be with child and
bring forth a son, and they shall call his name
Emmanuel, which being interpreted is God with us.

In those days came John the Baptist, preaching
in the wilderness of Judaea and saying, Repent:
for the kingdom of heaven is at hand. This is he
that was spoken of by the prophet Esaias [Isaiah],
saying, The voice of one crying in the wilderness,

Prepare ye the way of the Lord, make his paths straight.

Seeing the multitudes, he [Jesus] went up into a mountain: when he was set, his disciples came unto him: and he opened his mouth and taught them.

Lay not up for yourselves treasures upon earth, where moth and rust corrupts and where thieves break through and steal: but lay up for yourselves treasures in heaven, where neither moth nor rust doth corrupt and where thieves do not break through nor steal: for where your treasure is, there will your heart be also.

Enter in at the strait gate: for wide is the gate and broad the way that leadeth to destruction, and many go in thereat: strait is the gate and narrow the way which leadeth to life, and few find it.

Whosoever heareth these sayings of mine and doeth them, I will liken him unto a wise man which built his house upon a rock: the rain descended, the floods came, and the winds blew and beat upon that house; and it fell not: for it was founded upon a rock.

When Jesus had ended these sayings, the people

were astonished: for he taught as one having authority, and not as the scribes.

Jesus went about all the cities and villages, teaching in their synagogues, preaching the gospel of the kingdom, and healing every sickness and disease among the people.

When he saw the multitudes, he was moved with compassion on them, because they fainted and were scattered abroad, as sheep having no shepherd. Then saith he unto his disciples, The harvest is plenteous, but the labourers are few; pray therefore the Lord of the harvest, that he will send forth labourers into his harvest.

From that time forth began Jesus to shew unto his disciples how he must go unto Jerusalem, suffer many things of the elders and chief priests and scribes, be killed, and be raised again the third day.

Then Peter began to rebuke him, saying, Be it far from thee, Lord: this shall not be unto thee.

But he said unto Peter, Get behind me, Satan: thou art an offence unto me: for thou savourest not the things of God, but those of men.

# MARK

Jesus took again the twelve and began to tell
them what things should happen unto him,
saying, Behold, we go up to Jerusalem; and the
Son of man shall be delivered unto the chief
priests and scribes; they shall condemn him to
death and deliver him to the Gentiles: they shall
mock him, scourge him, spit upon him, and kill
him: and the third day he shall rise again.

When they came nigh to Jerusalem, unto
Bethphage and Bethany, at the mount of Olives,
he sendeth forth two of his disciples and saith
unto them, Go into the village over against you:
as soon as ye enter it, ye shall find a colt tied,
whereon never man sat; loose him and bring him.
And if any man say, Why do ye this? say that the
Lord hath need of him; and straightway he will
send him.

They brought the colt to Jesus and cast their
garments on him; and he sat upon him. Many
spread their garments in the way: others cut
branches off the trees and strawed them in
the way. They that went before and they that
followed cried, Hosanna to the son of David:

Blessed is he that cometh in the name of the Lord; Hosanna in the highest. Jesus entered into Jerusalem and into the temple: when he had looked round about upon all things and eventide was come, he went out unto Bethany with the twelve.

As he sat upon the mount of Olives over against the temple, Peter and James and John and Andrew asked him privately, Tell us, when shall these things be? and what shall be the sign when all these things shall be fulfilled?

Jesus began to say, Take heed lest any man deceive you: for many shall come in my name, saying, I am Christ; and shall deceive many. And when ye hear of wars and rumours of wars, be not troubled: for such things must be; but the end shall not be yet.

## LUKE

Now the feast of unleavened bread drew nigh, which is called the Passover. The chief priests and scribes sought how they might kill him [Jesus]; for they feared the people.

Then entered Satan into Judas Iscariot, being of the number of the twelve. He went his way and communed with the chief priests and captains, how he might betray him unto them.

Jesus went to the mount of Olives; and his disciples followed him. When he was at the place, he said unto them, Pray that ye enter not into temptation.

He was withdrawn from them about a stone's cast, and kneeled down and prayed, saying, Father, if thou be willing, remove this cup from me: nevertheless not my will, but thine, be done. There appeared an angel unto him from heaven, strengthening him. Being in an agony he prayed more earnestly: and his sweat was as it were great drops of blood falling to the ground.

While he yet spake, behold a multitude, and Judas, one of the twelve, went before them and drew near unto Jesus to kiss him. But Jesus said, Judas, betrayest thou the Son of man with a kiss?

Then Jesus said unto the chief priests, captains of the temple, and elders, which were come to him, Be ye come out as against a thief, with swords and staves? When I was daily with you in the temple, ye stretched forth no hands against me: but this is your hour and the power of darkness. Then took they him and brought him into the high priest's house.

As soon as it was day, the elders of the people and

the chief priests and scribes came together and led him into their council, saying, Art thou the Christ? tell us.

He said unto them, If I tell you, ye will not believe: and if I also ask you, ye will not answer me, nor let me go. Hereafter shall the Son of man sit on the right hand of the power of God.

Then said they all, Art thou then the Son of God?

He said, Ye say that I am.

They said, What need we any further witness? for we ourselves have heard of his own mouth.

Pilate, when he had called together the chief priests and the rulers and the people, said, Ye have brought this man unto me as one that perverteth the people: behold, I, having examined him before you, have found no fault in this man touching those things whereof ye accuse him.

They were instant with loud voices, requiring that he might be crucified. And the voices of them and of the chief priests prevailed. Pilate gave sentence that it should be as they required. He released unto them him that for sedition and murder was cast into prison, whom they had desired; but he delivered Jesus to their will.

As they led him away, they laid hold upon one Simon, a Cyrenian, coming out of the country, and on him they laid the cross, that he might bear it after Jesus. There were also two malefactors led with him to be put to death. When they were come to the place called Calvary, there they crucified him and the malefactors, one on the right hand and the other on the left. Then said Jesus, Father, forgive them; for they know not what they do.

It was about the sixth hour, and there was a darkness over all the earth until the ninth hour. The sun was darkened, and the veil of the temple was rent. When Jesus had cried with a loud voice, he said, Father, into thy hands I commend my spirit: having said thus, he gave up the ghost.

## JOHN

After this Joseph of Arimathaea, being a disciple of Jesus, besought Pilate that he might take away the body of Jesus: and Pilate gave him leave. He came therefore and took the body of Jesus. There came also Nicodemus, which at the first came to Jesus by night.

They took the body of Jesus and wound it in linen clothes with spices, as the manner of the Jews is to bury. Now in the place where he was crucified there was a garden; and in the garden a new sepulchre, wherein was never man yet laid.

There laid they Jesus therefore because of the Jews' preparation day.

The first day of the week cometh Mary Magdalene early, when it was yet dark, unto the sepulchre, and seeth the stone taken away. She runneth to Simon Peter and the other disciple, whom Jesus loved, and saith to them, They have taken the Lord out of the sepulchre, and we know not where they have laid him.

Mary stood at the sepulchre weeping: and as she wept, she stooped down and looked into the sepulchre and seeth two angels in white sitting, one at the head, the other at the feet, where the body of Jesus had lain. They say unto her, Woman, why weepest thou?

She saith unto them, Because they have taken away my Lord, and I know not where they have laid him. When she had thus said, she turned and saw Jesus standing, and knew not that it was Jesus.

Jesus saith unto her, Woman, why weepest thou? whom seekest thou?

She, supposing him to be the gardener, saith unto him, Sir, if thou have borne him hence, tell me where thou hast laid him, and I will take him away.

Jesus saith unto her, Mary.

She turned and saith, Rabboni; which is to say, Master.

Jesus saith, Touch me not; for I am not yet ascended to my Father: but go to my brethren, and say unto them, I ascend unto my Father and your Father; to my God and your God.

Mary Magdalene told the disciples that she had seen the Lord and that he had spoken these things unto her.

Then the same day at evening, being the first day of the week, when the doors were shut where the disciples were assembled for fear of the Jews, came Jesus and stood in the midst and saith, Peace be unto you. When he had so said, he shewed them his hands and his side. Then were the disciples glad when they saw the Lord. Then said Jesus to them again, Peace be unto you: as my Father hath sent me, even so send I you.

# ACTS OF THE APOSTLES

Jesus, being assembled together with them, commanded them that they should not depart from Jerusalem, but wait for the promise of the Father, which ye have heard of me. For John truly baptized with water; but ye shall be baptized with the Holy Ghost not many days hence.

They asked, Lord, wilt thou at this time restore again the kingdom to Israel?

He said, It is not for you to know the times or the seasons, which the Father hath put in his own power. But ye shall receive power after the Holy Ghost is come upon you: and ye shall be witnesses unto me in Jerusalem and in all Judaea and in Samaria, unto the uttermost part of the earth.

When he had spoken these things, while they beheld, he was taken up; and a cloud received him out of their sight.

When the day of Pentecost was fully come, they were all with one accord in one place. Suddenly there came a sound from heaven as of a rushing mighty wind, and it filled the house where they were sitting. There appeared unto them cloven tongues as of fire, and it sat upon each of them. They were all filled with the Holy Ghost and began to speak with other tongues as the Spirit gave them utterance.

Peter, standing with the eleven, lifted up his voice and said, Men of Judaea and all that dwell at Jerusalem, be this known unto you, and hearken to my words: For these are not drunken, as ye suppose, seeing it is but the third hour of the day. But this is that which was spoken by the prophet Joel; And it shall come to pass in the last days, saith God, I will pour out my Spirit upon all flesh: your sons and daughters shall prophesy, your young men shall see visions, and your old men shall dream dreams.

When they had prayed, the place was shaken where they were assembled; they were all filled with the Holy Ghost and spake the word of God with boldness. The multitude of them that believed were of one heart and one soul: neither said any of them that ought of the things he possessed was his own; but they had all things common. With great power gave the apostles witness of the resurrection of the Lord Jesus: and great grace was upon them all.

Saul, yet breathing out threatenings and slaughter against the disciples of the Lord, went unto the high priest and desired of him letters to Damascus to the synagogues, that if he found any of this way, whether men or women, he might bring them bound unto Jerusalem.

As he journeyed, he came near Damascus: and suddenly there shined round him a light from heaven: he fell to the earth and heard a voice saying unto him, Saul, Saul, why persecutest me?

He said, Who art thou, Lord?

And the Lord said, I am Jesus whom thou persecutest: it is hard for thee to kick against the pricks.

And he trembling and astonished said, Lord, what wilt thou have me to do?

The Lord said, Arise, go into the city, and it shall be told thee what thou must do.

There was a certain disciple at Damascus named Ananias; to him said the Lord in a vision, Ananias.

He said, Behold, I am here, Lord.

The Lord said unto him, Arise, go into the street called Straight, and enquire in the house of Judas for one called Saul, of Tarsus: for, behold, he prayeth and hath seen in a vision a man named Ananias coming in and putting his hand on him, that he might receive his sight.

Ananias answered, Lord, I have heard by many of this man, how much evil he hath done to thy saints at Jerusalem.

But the Lord said unto him, Go thy way: for he is a chosen vessel unto me, to bear my name before the Gentiles and kings and the children of Israel.

Saul, (who is also called Paul,) testified the kingdom of God, persuading them concerning Jesus, both out of the law of Moses and out of the prophets.

# ROMANS

Paul, a servant of Jesus Christ, called to be an apostle, separated unto the gospel of God. I am not ashamed of the gospel of Christ: for it is the power of God unto salvation to every one that believeth; to the Jew first and also to the Greek.

Therein is the righteousness of God revealed from faith to faith: as it is written, The just shall live by faith. For the wrath of God is revealed from heaven against all ungodliness and unrighteousness of men.

The righteousness of God is by faith of Jesus Christ unto all and upon all that believe: there is no difference: for all have sinned and come short of the glory of God; being justified freely by his grace through the redemption that is in Christ Jesus.

What shall we say then that Abraham our father, as pertaining to the flesh, hath found? For if Abraham were justified by works, he hath whereof to glory; but not before God. For what saith the scripture? Abraham believed God, and it was counted unto him for righteousness. Being justified by faith, we have peace with God through our Lord Jesus Christ: by whom also we have access by faith into this grace wherein we stand, and rejoice in hope of the glory of God. Not only so, but we glory in tribulations also: knowing that tribulation worketh patience; patience, experience; and experience, hope: and hope maketh not ashamed; because the love of God is shed abroad in our hearts by the Holy Ghost given unto us.

# 1 Corinthians

Paul, called to be an apostle of Jesus Christ through the will of God, unto the church of God at Corinth: Grace be unto you from God our Father and the Lord Jesus Christ. I beseech you, brethren, by the name of our Lord Jesus Christ, that ye all speak the same thing and that there be no divisions among you; but that ye be perfectly joined together in the same mind and the same judgment.

I, brethren, when I came to you, came not with excellency of speech or of wisdom, declaring unto you the testimony of God. For I determined not to know any thing among you, save Jesus Christ and him crucified. My speech and preaching was not with enticing words of man's wisdom, but in demonstration of the Spirit and of power: that your faith should not stand in the wisdom of men but in the power of God.

Be followers of me even as I also am of Christ. I praise you, brethren, that ye remember me in all things and keep the ordinances as I delivered them to you.

Thanks be to God, which giveth us victory

through our Lord Jesus Christ. Therefore, my beloved brethren, be stedfast, unmoveable, always abounding in the work of the Lord, as ye know that your labour is not in vain in the Lord.

## 2 CORINTHIANS

We know that if our earthly house of this tabernacle were dissolved, we have a building of God, a house not made with hands, eternal in the heavens. For in this we groan, earnestly desiring to be clothed with our house which is from heaven: if so being clothed we shall not be found naked. For we that are in this tabernacle do groan, being burdened: not that we would be unclothed, but clothed, that mortality might be swallowed up of life. Now he that hath wrought us for the selfsame thing is God, who also hath given us the earnest of the Spirit. Therefore we are always confident, knowing that whilst we are at home in the body, we are absent from the Lord: (For we walk by faith, not by sight:) We are confident, I say, and willing rather to be absent from the body and present with the Lord.

If any man be in Christ, he is a new creature: old things are passed away; all things are become new.

# GALATIANS

Paul, an apostle, and all the brethren with me, unto the churches of Galatia. I marvel that ye are so soon removed from him that called you into the grace of Christ unto another gospel: which is not another; but there be some that trouble you and would pervert the gospel of Christ. But though we or an angel from heaven preach any other gospel unto you than that which we have preached, let him be accursed.

# EPHESIANS

Paul, an apostle of Jesus by the will of God, to the saints at Ephesus and to the faithful in Christ: By grace are ye saved through faith; it is the gift of God: Not of works, lest any man should boast.

Walk worthy of the vocation wherewith ye are called, with all lowliness and meekness, with longsuffering, forbearing one another in love; endeavoring to keep the unity of the Spirit in the bond of peace.

Be strong in the Lord and in the power of his might.

# PHILIPPIANS

Paul and Timotheus, servants of Jesus Christ, to all the saints in Philippi: Rejoice in the Lord always: again I say, Rejoice. Let your moderation be known unto all. The Lord is at hand. Be careful for nothing; but in every thing by prayer and supplication with thanksgiving let your requests be made known unto God. And the peace of God, which passeth all understanding, shall keep your hearts and minds through Christ Jesus.

# COLOSSIANS

Paul, an apostle of Jesus to the saints and brethren at Colosse: If ye be risen with Christ, seek those things which are above, where Christ sitteth on the right hand of God. Set your affection on things above, not on things on the earth. For ye are dead, and your life is hid with Christ in God. When Christ, who is our life, shall appear, then shall ye also appear with him in glory.

# 1 Thessalonians

Paul, and Silvanus, and Timotheus, unto the church of the Thessalonians: We which are alive and remain unto the coming of the Lord shall not prevent them which are asleep. For the Lord himself shall descend from heaven with a shout, with the voice of the archangel, and with the trump of God: the dead in Christ shall rise first: then we which are alive and remain shall be caught up together with them in the clouds to meet the Lord in the air.

# 2 Thessalonians

Brethren, pray for us, that the word of the Lord may have free course and be glorified, even as it is with you: and that we may be delivered from unreasonable and wicked men.

# 1 Timothy

Paul unto Timothy, my own son in the faith. This

is a faithful saying and worthy of all acceptation, that Christ Jesus came into the world to save sinners; of whom I am chief. Howbeit for this cause I obtained mercy, that in me first Jesus Christ might shew forth all longsuffering, for a pattern to them which should hereafter believe on him to life everlasting. Now unto the King eternal, immortal, invisible, the only wise God, be honour and glory for ever and ever.

## 2 TIMOTHY

God hath saved us and called us with an holy calling, not according to our works, but according to his own purpose and grace, which was given us in Christ Jesus before the world began, but is now made manifest by the appearing of our Saviour Jesus Christ, who hath abolished death and brought life and immortality to light through the gospel.

All scripture is given by inspiration of God, and is profitable for doctrine, reproof, correction, instruction in righteousness: That the man of God may be thoroughly furnished unto good works.

## TITUS

Paul, servant of God, to Titus, mine own son after the faith: The grace of God that bringeth salvation hath appeared to all men, teaching us that, denying ungodliness and worldly lusts, we should live soberly, righteously, and godly in this present world.

## PHILEMON

Paul unto Philemon: I beseech thee for Onesimus in time past unprofitable, but now profitable to thee and to me: Receive him not now as a servant, but a brother beloved.

## HEBREWS

Let us labour to enter into that rest, lest any man fall after the same example of unbelief. For the word of God is quick, powerful, and sharper than any two-edged sword, piercing even to the dividing asunder of soul and spirit, and is a discerner of the thoughts and intents of the heart.

Let us therefore come boldly unto the throne of grace, that we may obtain mercy and find grace to help in time of need.

Let us draw near with a true heart in full assurance of faith, having our hearts sprinkled from an evil conscience and our bodies washed with pure water. Let us hold fast the profession of our faith without wavering; and let us consider one another to provoke unto love and good works.

Seeing we are compassed about with so great a cloud of witnesses, let us lay aside every weight and the sin which doth so easily beset us, and let us run with patience the race that is set before us, looking unto Jesus the author and finisher of our faith.

## JAMES

James, a servant of God and the Lord Jesus Christ, to the twelve tribes scattered abroad. Brethren, count it all joy when ye fall into divers temptations; knowing that the trying of your faith worketh patience. But let patience have her perfect work, that ye may be perfect and entire, wanting nothing.

The effectual fervent prayer of a righteous man availeth much.

# 1 PETER

Peter, apostle of Jesus Christ, to the elect: Blessed be the God and Father of our Lord Jesus Christ: whom having not seen, ye love; in whom ye rejoice with joy unspeakable and full of glory: receiving the end of your faith, even the salvation of your souls.

Forasmuch as Christ hath suffered for us in the flesh, arm yourselves likewise with the same mind: for he that suffered in the flesh hath ceased from sin; that he no longer should live his time in the flesh to the lusts of men, but to the will of God.

# 2 PETER

His divine power hath given us all things that pertain unto life and godliness through the knowledge of him that hath called us to glory and virtue: whereby are given unto us exceeding great and precious promises: that by these ye might be partakers of the divine nature, having escaped the corruption that is in the world through lust.

The Lord is not slack concerning his promise, as some men count slackness; but is longsuffering, not willing that any should perish but that all should come to repentance. The day of the Lord will come as a thief in the night; the heavens shall pass away with a great noise, and the elements shall melt with fervent heat, the earth and the works that are therein shall be burned.

## 1 JOHN

That which we have seen and heard declare we unto you, that ye also may have fellowship with us: truly our fellowship is with the Father and his Son Jesus Christ.

My little children, these things write I to you that ye sin not. If any man sin, we have an advocate with the Father, Jesus Christ the righteous: he is the propitiation for our sins.

## 2 JOHN

The elder unto the elect lady. Not as though I wrote a new commandment, but that which we had from the beginning, love one another.

## 3 JOHN

The elder unto the well-beloved Gaius. I have no greater joy than to hear that my children walk in truth.

## JUDE

Jude, to them that are preserved in Jesus Christ. Ye should earnestly contend for the faith which was once delivered unto the saints. Keep yourselves in the love of God.

## REVELATION

The Revelation of Jesus Christ, which God gave unto him to shew his servants things which must shortly come to pass; he sent and signified it by his angel unto his servant John. Blessed is he that readeth and they that hear the words of this prophecy and keep those things written therein: for the time is at hand.

I was in the Spirit on the Lord's day and heard behind me a great voice, as of a trumpet, saying, I am Alpha and Omega, the first and the last: and, What thou seest, write in a book, and send it unto the seven churches in Asia; unto Ephesus, Smyrna, Pergamos, Thyatira, Sardis, Philadelphia, and Laodicea.

These sayings are faithful and true: and the Lord God of the holy prophets sent his angel to shew unto his servants the things which must shortly be done. Blessed is he that keepeth the sayings of the prophecy of this book. Behold, I come quickly; and my reward is with me, to give every man according as his work shall be.

Blessed are they that do his commandments, that they may have right to the tree of life and may enter in through the gates into the city. For without are dogs, sorcerers, whoremongers, murderers, idolaters, and whosoever loveth and maketh a lie.

I Jesus have sent mine angel to testify unto you these things in the churches. I am the root and the offspring of David, the bright and morning star. The Spirit and the bride say, Come. Let him that heareth say, Come. And let him that is athirst come. Whosoever will, let him take the water of life freely.